Just A
Closer Walking
Devotional

Shalonda "Treasure" Williams

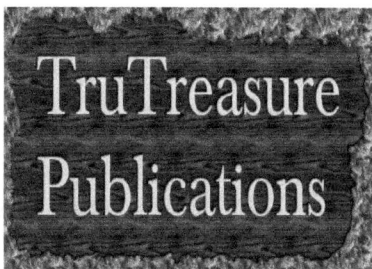

TruTreasure
Publications

For My Grandmothers
Marie Meadows
Eva Mae Parker
Daisy Williams

God only knows the lessons that I've learned from wise women like yourselves. Thank you all for contributing to the make up of me! Rest in beautiful peace.

Day 1

Salvation....

Before I go any further, let's just say the following prayer statement aloud.

Father God, Maker of heaven and earth, I come to you presenting my heart, mind and body. I come to confess with my mouth that I believe in my heart that you have raised Jesus Christ from the dead. I believe that he is now seated in heavenly places with You at Your right hand and that one day he will return. I ask that you forgive me for all sins that are known to me and even the ones that are unknown. Please forgive those things that I have done wrong against You, Oh God, and anyone else. I repent, meaning I willing turn away from practicing those things that I know are not pleasing to You. I pray that You would arrest my mind. Teach me your ways Oh Lord that I may walk according to Your plan for me. In and through Jesus' Name. Amen.

Well, yes indeed! It is now finished for you. I pray that your heart was truly in that. It could have served as your very first dish of receiving Christ or it could have been a statement of re-dedication. Either way we are on the right track and we will continue on from here.

Below you will find your daily scriptures to read. But, don't just read them. Pray and allow God to really help you see and embody what you read throughout this challenge. #ThinkOnTheseThings

Daily Scriptures:

1 John 5: 11-12
Romans 10: 9-10
Philippians 3: 8-11
Hebrews 7:25

(Don't forget to write down all thoughts and questions. Nothing is a stupid question. Prepare your heart and mind to receive answers from the Lord)

Day 2

Salvation is more than...

Now that we have gone before the Lord in repentance and in order to accept Jesus Christ as our Lord and Savior, we must go further. It is my intent on this day to shed a little more light on salvation. The word *salvation,* according to google, means preservation or deliverance from harm, ruin, or loss.

I bring up the definition in order to show you that salvation is an on-going thing. Even as we are pursuing a closer walk with God, there will be times when we still need to cry out for salvation or deliverance. It is okay to need your Father to rescue you. It is okay to say that you need Him.

Often times, when we are going through we shut down. All of a sudden our voices seem to leave us and we get silent... even with God. We cry at times and then we tend to hide in a corner. This is the WRONG thing to do. It is during these times that our conversation with God should grow by leaps and bounds. As humans, we often get upset with those who are not ashamed to speak up. Most of us, at some point in life or another, have gotten to be unfamiliar with how to effectively communicate what we need.

Today, I want you to reevaluate your communication. Do you communicate with our God or do you shut down and just expect Him to get it? Yes, I know that we know Him as a sovereign God and we know that He knows all things, yet, we must give voice to things. He wants to hear from You. If you need Him to rescue you or deliver you from something, tell Him. That's what a relationship is all about. Silence, when it comes to our God, is not golden. Just ask King David and the psalmist from scripture.

Salvation is more than just doing right until you get to heaven. God is our salvation all the time. Think about it, how can He give us salvation from sin, through the death of His Son, if He doesn't possess it already? #ThinkOnTheseThings

Daily Scriptures

Psalm 25
Psalm 71
Psalm 86: 16
Psalm 119: 146, 153
Philippians 4: 6

(Don't forget to take notes)

Day 3

Pray is communication...

On day 2 we talked about not allowing your communication with God to stop when you need to speak up and hear from Him the most. The communication in relationships are very strained in the world today. Everybody wants to prove their point and when that point is not heard we shut down even more. I can testify about being that way a time or two. But, I have learned over time that it is imperative to learn healthy communication and to keep the lines open.

So, what do we call communication with God? We call it prayer. Prayer is used for petitioning, showing adoration and even giving thanks. It is the way we tell God that we need Him. With it we let Father know how much we honor Him. We also tell Him how thankful we are, even in the smallest matters. It is our way of communicating with Our Creator.

We all know that with no form of communication a relationship of any kind will die. Marriages fall apart, children feel unloved and abandoned, business partnerships dissolve and friendships wane with the lack of communication.

Let's define the word communication. One of

the definitions that google gives says, "The means of connection between people or places". Wow. So, do you mean to tell me that I am connected to God through my prayers? Yes, that's exactly what I am saying. Because prayer is our way of communicating with Him, then prayer creates a connection, if done from a pure place.

Your task for today is to really reflect on what it means to have a connection with someone. What does it take to create one? What does it take to maintain it? And, what can break it? Since your goal is to have a closer walk then wouldn't it behoove you to examine these questions in a deeper way? #ThinkOnTheseThings

Daily Scriptures

James 4: 2-3
1 Thessalonians 5: 16-18
Jeremiah 29: 12-13
Proverbs 28: 9
1 John 5: 14
Psalm 18: 6

Day 4

Prayers of Petition...

Now that we have talked about the importance of having and keeping a connection with God through prayer, we are going to take a few days to talk about the different types of prayer. First, I want to dive into what it means to petition God. You also need to know that it is not a bad thing to do so. Many of us have lost our voice when it comes to petitioning because of old talk coming from those who were influenced by people who just didn't know any better. It's all good right now though because we are going to shine light in the dark places so that you can be liberated and no longer afraid to ask.

The word petition is speaking of an urgent request that is made to God, but in a very humble and reverential way. Some other words that are used by Bible Hub are: solicit, supplication, entreat or simply to ask. This is the prayer where we ask God for the things that we need or desire. We solicit His help in times of hardship.

Have you ever been in need and you decided to pray to God to fulfill this need? I have, of course, on more than one occasion, been in this type situation. I wrote of one of the times in my book,

From Trash To Treasure. This petition was for something I desperately needed. Deliverance. I was in a place in my life where I could have gotten deeper and deeper if I had not cried out with all my heart to be free. This plea, was from such a real place.

It is okay for you to solicit God's help in your life when you are living upright before Him. It is also okay for you to cry out for deliverance and salvation. Make your request known unto God. This is one of very powerful benefits of serving Him. #ThinkOnTheseThings

Daily Scriptures

Psalm 20: 4-6
Philippians 4:6
James 1: 5-6
Psalm 17: 6
John 11: 42

Day 5

Prayers For Others

Prayers for others or "standing in the gap" for others is what is called a prayer of intercession. Many of us have heard of an intercessor. A person, most often, at our places of worship who stands before the congregation and prays heaven down. Lol. They often pray for everything from the pastors to the smallest baby. They send up petitions on behalf of others, they bind and cast down spirits and they even cover the service for the day or evening.

Prayers of intercession reach the heart of God, especially when they are made from the heart of someone that truly has a heart for others, ministry or just the kingdom of God as a whole. This is also exactly what Jesus Christ does for us on a consistence basis. He is seated at the right hand of the Father making intercession for us.

To be one who intercedes puts an individual in a very selfless place. True intercession must be done from a pure place. Now, the question that many may ask is, "Do I have to be named an intercessor to be able to pray for others?" The short answer to that is absolutely not. The longer answer to that is this...

...When your loved one is in trouble, your child or parent is ill, or when your friend is hurting from a heartbreak, do you wait for permission to pray for them? Probably not.

The truth is that even if you solicit the prayers of someone that you believe is more "qualified" to pray, you have more than likely already said sent up some level of a plea to God on their behalf. Now, of course, there is nothing wrong with asking for someone else to touch and agree with you for them, but, because you are also in right standing with God, having received salvation, you, too, are qualified to intercede.

So, when you feel that urge to pray for someone you love and you don't feel like you can, ask yourself, "Why not me"? There are many examples of intercession in the scriptures. Explore them why don't you. #ThinkOnTheseThings

Daily Scriptures

1 Thessalonians 1: 11-12
Ephesians 1: 15-19
Philippians 1: 9-11
Colossians 1: 9-12
John 17: 21

Day 6

Prayer That Offer Thanks To God

Do we truly know just how worthy God is of all honor, glory, praise and thanks? I don't always think that we do. Really. I spend time thinking about myself even. Shalonda, do you understand how graced you are and how much God has shielded you from so many catastrophes? I honestly evaluate this and then I begin to go into prayers of thanksgiving and even a round of tears.

For many who have followed me or Love Walk Outreach for any length of time, you may have heard me speak on my life and the many irresponsible choices I have made. Being promiscuous was one of the biggest ones. By the age of 13 I was no longer a virgin, but even before that I had been touched and fondled. By the time I was 18 years old my count was way above normal. Nothing I am proud of now but at the time I was experiencing all types of feelings and emotions. Nevertheless, no matter my reasons at the time, it was so unsafe.

There were those that I grew up with that did not have nearly as many sexual encounters as I'd had that ended up in some bad situations. Some were parents before we had gotten to our sophomore year in high school. Others lived in the clinic due to the fact that they acquired multiple STDs over the course of a few years or even months. There was even a young lady that I went to college with that was diagnosed with HIV after only her first time having sex. These were some very unfortunate circumstances.

You would think that after hearing these things or watching my friends become parents earlier than expected, that I would have slowed down. I did not. I was just as bad, if not worse, until I got pregnant at 19 years old. Even then, it was the having a baby to care for that made me stop searching for that "fix" a little less.

I shared that tid bit of my story to say that I KNOW without a shadow of a doubt that I am blessed beyond measure. I KNOW that God has had His hand upon my life and that He has watched over me with a special eye. So many possible outcomes could have come upon me. Including premature death. So, now that I am on this side of that stronghold, I made a choice that every time I think about it I WILL THANK HIM. I will get beside myself in thanking Him because things could have surely been the other way around.

I will challenge you this day to get you a thanksgiving prayer journal. Everyday jot down, at least, 5 things that you are grateful for. Make it a habit. The more you do this, the more it gets stuck or ingrained in your spiritual DNA. After you write them down, speak them out of your mouth.

Make giving thanks a lifestyle.
#ThinkOnTheseThings

Daily Scriptures

Philippians 4: 6
Colossians 4: 2
1 Thessalonians 5: 16-18

Day 7

Making Great Use of The Model Prayer

Matthew 6: 9-13 holds our focus for today. Here I am going to write it for sake of what I want to do. I would like to show you these verses each in their place. Line by line so that you can get a clear picture of what I believe that Jesus was trying to show us.

According to Bible Gateway's KJV it is written as such:

"**9** *After this manner therefore pray ye:*
Our Father which art in heaven, Hallowed be thy name."

Jesus starts by telling his disciples to pray according to his example. He begins with first things first. He honors God the Father. Reverence is a must to Him. He deserves it and He and His name is indeed Holy (hallowed).

"**10** *Thy kingdom come, Thy will be done in earth, as it is in heaven.*"

This prayer goes on to beckon God's kingdom to come and set up here in the earth with us as it already exists in heaven. Jesus is telling them to ask for and even anticipate God's way of doing things and governing to be where we are. We have heard how some places in the world have kingdoms and how they are ran yet we know not fully how God wants things to be. It is what we should be seeking.

"11 *Give us this day our daily bread.*"

This verse is something that many of us are afraid to say and truly mean. This is a statement of faith. In this we are telling God that we trust Him for our day to day provision. This is not speaking to a far off day. It is believing that each and every day God will provide, even if you can not see how He can or will do it.

"12 *And forgive us our debts, as we forgive our debtors.*"

Verse 12 is not just talking about forgiving a person of their trespasses or sins against you. That is a part of it but it is also talking about literal debt. Are you still holding on to when your "ex" friend borrowed $3 dollars? Or even when someone asked for a $100 loan? If so, forgive it. We are also asking God to forgive us of all things that we have done that would be considered debt to Him.

"**13** *And lead us not into temptation, but deliver us from evil: For thine is the kingdom, and the power, and the glory, for ever. Amen.*"

Of course, this verse speaks volumes in and of itself. We do not want to be tempted. We truly dislike being tempted because we don't really like to resist most of the things that come at us. God understands so here Jesus teaches us to ask God not to lead us into temptation but to deliver us. We also know that there is scripture that says that God will indeed provide a way of escape from temptation.

It goes on to say that God holds and possesses the kingdom, the power and the glory forever. And so it is.

My desire for you today is to take a closer look at the prayer that we have been praying all of our lives but not necessarily understanding. #ThinkOnTheseThings

Daily Scripture:

Reread Matthew 6: 9-13

Day 8

Praying With The Right Motives

How often do we pray and don't consider the motives with which we are praying? Are we praying with a greater whole in mind or are we simply praying to fulfill our selfish desires?

Some of us may actually take careful inventory and be honest and say that we, more often than not, pray with ourselves in my mind. It is the outcome that we see in or minds that we hope to see once we pray. Most will hurriedly answer this question and say, "Oh no, I pray with the greater things of God in mind". With that I will ask you to think again. Think very carefully before answering.

I challenge to reflect on the reason for your prayers. When you last prayed did you ramble on about all that you wanted to have in order to fulfill the lust of your flesh. When I say the lust of our flesh I am talking everyday life things that we use to tantalize our senses. In themselves the things we take possession of while here on earth are not an awful thing. The problem comes in when we pray for these things and we don't get them and the lack thereof causes us to be emotional and even makes us feel incomplete.

Do you pray desperate prayers for things that

please the flesh only, such as belongings, for God to send you a spouse, for that brand new car with every detail you can think of or for more money than you can count? Again, these things in themselves would not appear to be a problem. You may be reading this right now thinking, "Why is she making it seem that having the things I desire is a problem?" I really don't want you to feel that way.

What we, as humans, tend to do is forget that there is nothing worth having more than having God and His kingdom. Throughout scripture this is almost drilled into us. Things became idols and God even spoke of being a jealous God because it became so normal for the people.

What I am trying to get through to you is that your prayers should always be prayed with first things first. God's will is what we should be seeking. When we pray for His will to be done and we actually mean it, we open ourselves up for so much more than we could ever ask or think. Even when we petition God for the things we desire, it should be from a perspective that says, "Father, if it be your will...". This way, if He choices not to give it, you are okay and will not fall into a pit of despair.

Also, all of our prayers should be unto God and not to be seen. We, in this day and time, pray in public, however, it should never be to be seen by anyone. Doing anything just to get attention will always cause a not so favorable outcome in the long run. #ThinkOnTheseThings.

Daily Scriptures

Matthew 6: 5
James 4: 3

Day 9

Trusting God during the process

One of the things that I know for sure is that there are many people who get discouraged, and even hate when others say the famous line of, "Just pray on it and it will be okay". I giggle now thinking about how many women and even men I have had to say that to now and the response I get from them. In times like these we want to hear nice, fluffy things that make us feel better about what we are going through.

Quickly, tell me when "pray and everything will be okay" became a bad thing though?

Anyway, the nice things that we want to hear are often times things that are laced with lies that pacify us. This is not what we need during times of processing a.k.a hardships. It is a time of processing if during yours days, you are tired and feeling weary and during your nights you are tossing and turning. Processing is not the easiest thing to endure and can feel very much like a weight upon your back and shoulders.

Some examples of times of processing could be healing after a divorce, fighting depression after the loss of a loved one, or even fighting fear and worry after losing a job because no other prospects seem to be in sight. It seems that these things, and more, happen right after you have been told that great and marvelous things are going to happen in your life. So, the process seems horrific. It breaks you down in ways you did not think possible.

YET, this is the time where faith shows itself. Have you ever been told that faith without works is dead? So, what if the works is to have joy and to praise even in the midst of the processing?

God has given us tools in the scriptures that we are to apply to our lives in times like these. Some of those scriptures have been given to you in the previous days challenge. It is very important that you begin to seek out how God desires for you to go through. The biggest thing He wants is for us to continue to trust Him throughout the entire process that we are undergoing.

It is not easy to praise God pass our emotions. It is even harder for a person who is used to putting trust only in themselves, to turn around in put their trust in a God they can not see. However, this is an essential step to having a closer walk with God. The process may hurt, leave you sad, or break your heart, but you can do this. Seek Him and listen closely to His voice. #ThinkOnTheseThings

Daily Scriptures:

Proverbs 3:5
2 Samuel 7: 28
Psalm 9: 10
Psalm 20: 7

32

Day 10

Renewing My Mind

(Taken From Upcoming Book "Flip My Mind: Coaching Myself To Spiritual Maturity" by Shalonda "Treasure" Williams)

Everyone that I come into contact with that are "Christians" and even some that have any believing friends, know the scripture that speaks of "Being transformed by the renewing of your mind". It is a very popular scripture because it speaks of all we think we know from our upbringing or what life has taught us and the fact that it needs to be adjusted. It talks of how the renewing of our minds is essential to being able to show forth what is truly acceptable to God.

Having to renew our minds doesn't seem too hard in concept but the work of doing so is hard indeed. It is even harder when a person simply does not want to let go of the corrupted mindset. These mindsets that we carry around are the true dictator of our life's happenings. We just don't get that but it is truth. When our minds have taken in so much that is against God's way and will, we live life on terms that can not keep us covered. Until we can change the way we think and allow ourselves to be transformed into the daughter/son that God knows we can be, we will always go in circles. We will be hit with the same tests over and over again; the same or very similar life struggles.

The word *renewed*, according to google, has a few different meanings but they all flow together. There it means to re-establish, replace, resume, restart, etc. In this verse it to be transformed by the re-establishing of a relationship with The Most High. It is to replace the old way of thinking with God's way of thinking. Also, it is to resume or restart your mind to seeking what it was once looking for in God. My goodness that's good.

So, what are we waiting for? Why is it so hard to give up the things that keep failing us in life? #ThinkOnTheseThings

Daily Scriptures

Romans 12: 2
Ephesians 4: 23
John 8: 32
Philippians 2: 5

Day 11

Change Your Focus

I went on Facebook live a while ago with the intention of talking about the bloodline patterns that we pass on to our children. Speaking of fighting against them and breaking generational curses. I was on a prayer call with Prophet Adebayo Isacc Ojo and he was speaking some real truths about how we continue to let patterns remain. He said "Even when we die our children are still left to fight the bloodline pattern and curses". It was a great teaching and it sparked something in me that I was inspired to talk about. BUTTTTTT... lol, I got on there and in my ear I had playing "Here in Our Praise" by United Tenors. My my my the praise that rose out of me was so liberating. This praise led to a whole other Facebook live message.

God begin to speak to the people listening. Through me He spoke of changing our focus to what we can give to Him instead always worrying about what He can give to us. We already know that there is so much that He gives to us, starting with our very breath. We complain so much about all we don't have yet we fail to see pass all of what is not to all of what is.

Needless to say, God wants our focus. He wants our praise, admiration and worship. So, the question is, what if we truly change our focus to what we can give unto Him. The scriptures tell us that it is more blessed to give than to receive. If this is indeed true then that means that God can take the principle of giving and make it to where you never know lack because you are so busy giving out that you don't even notice how much God keeps pouring back in. Hallelujah! #ThinkOnTheseThings

Daily Scriptures:

Philippians 4: 7-8
Colossians 3: 2
Acts 20: 35

Day 12

Entrusting God With Your Life

"My life is not my own, to you I belong. I give myself, I give myself to You." These are words from the song *I Give Myself Away* by William McDowell. We sing it all the time in praise and worship. We have it on our playlist that we jam to all the time. Yet.. Yet we don't really understand what it all means. Well, some do and some don't. Some just go through the motions of singing the song but have no real clue what they are saying to God.

This song makes real what Romans 12: 1-2 speaks of. Question? Are you truly ready to give yourself away to God? Presenting your body as a living sacrifice? Changing your mind to line up with the things of the spirit instead of what your flesh is telling you to do?

It is one thing to say it and a whole other thing to truly let go and let God.

There were so many throughout the scriptures that displayed this type of trust in God. Jesus, of course, is one of the greatest examples. Most of us know the story of the garden of Gethsemane when Jesus was hurting from taking on all the sins of the world. He was wanted the pain to stop yet he said to The Father, "Not as I will but your will be done".

This was amazing. He knew what was set before him. But he did not know what the process would feel like so when it came upon him, it was horrible. Yet and still he yield to Father.

Abraham did the same. He was instructed to leave all that was familiar to him and go to a place that he would not know until instructed. He was living with blind faith and God made him a great nation. Isaac was told to stay in a place that was in a famine. Not only was he told to stay but he was told to plant in the this famine. What he was doing didn't make since to those who were used to farming. Yet..... God showed up and showed out. Here is the thing however, it did 't come in a day. There was time in between the step of obedience and the reward. Can you handle that? Can you handle being so sold out to God that you would sow in the famine and then wait for God to bless it?

When we entrust our lives to God we say to Him, "I know that You know what is best and even when life seems to hate me in the midst of, I will still trust You." #ThinkOnTheseThings

Daily Scriptures

Luke 22: 42
Genesis 12: 1-4
Genesis 26: 1-12

Day 13

Submit to God

Following the course of yesterday I want to show you how you are to get to the point of entrusting your life and your whole self to God. It is a process called submission. The meaning of submit according to google is to *accept or yield to a superior force or to the authority or will of another person.* Another word for it is to yield. Just like yesterday, we talk today about letting God know that you are fully ready to yield to His plans for your life. The act of submitting to means that You indeed know what steps I should be taking and I take my will and put it out of mind so that Your plan can prevail.

There is one thing I love about God. He loves us so that He gave a choice. This submission He asks for is not forced. It is not something that He wants to drag out of us. The scriptures say to Submit to God. This in itself seems to be a tool for life living. It is given instructions on what we should do. This act alone can change the dynamics of our lives if we allow it to.

When the bible speaks of submitting, it is speaking of being under. And when I think of being God I think of being protected and covered.

To be submitted to God may not always feel that comfortable because there will be things that you do not understand. However, He is God and His plans are sure. He wants to us a great end just as he did for those that Jeremiah gave the word to. In their time of captivity and shame, God sent them a word. He told them to settle where they were. In other words, He was saying for them to learn to be content there but it would not be their ending. This goes with the scriptures when it tells us to be thankful in all things. That includes the uncomfortable situations that you may very well want to run from. My goodness I have a story or two to tell about that. LOL.

But, learning how to truly submit to God is about us learning to do things as He says. Obedience being greater than even your sacrifice. #ThinkOnTheseThings

Daily Scriptures:

Romans 8: 7
Romans 10: 3
James 4: 7

Day 14

Resist The Devil

This one statement right here is so jammed packed. I could say so much about it and give a lot of examples of how to this. I don't want to be long and drawn out with it though. We just have to know that this is one of the most vital parts of our walk. When people hear me talk about being intentional, this is much of where the intentional actions come in. This is a fight, not against flesh and blood but against Satan and his crew. They have their tactics and strategies and they use them. Why are we sitting here with weapons and still defeated?

When Jesus was in the wilderness being equipped for his earthly ministry Satan had to come to him. He was fasting and being endowed with power and the enemy had to come to see if he could get Jesus to fall and simply ignore what he has known thus far. The truth, that is. He was deliberate in what he offered our Savior to get him to fall prey. Riches, food, kingdoms, etc. Yet Jesus was intentional in every response he came to the devil.

Are you strategic in how you handle him? After the submission to God your mind should now be made up that when Satan comes you will not give in to any of his wiles and tricks. Giving my pearls away was my thing. There were so many times that I rationalized things in my mind about how that thing must have been God's will for me. It was ignorance.

I want to challenge you to make your resistance intentional. If your strong hold or your greatest temptation is sex, smoking cigarettes, stealing or any other addiction, RESIST.

When I was trying to remain celibate I had to turn off some TV programs and turn away from certain books. I had to suffer through the withdrawals. I had to ignore phone calls and doorbells. I even avoided men everywhere I would go so they wouldn't try to get at me. There was a spirit attached to me and I was cute too. Lol. They were like vultures, but God took me back and He was the most important factor. We must resist the enemies temptations to take us off of our righteous path. #ThinkOnTheseThings

Daily Scriptures:

James 4: 7
Luke 4: 1-13
Ephesians 4: 26-27

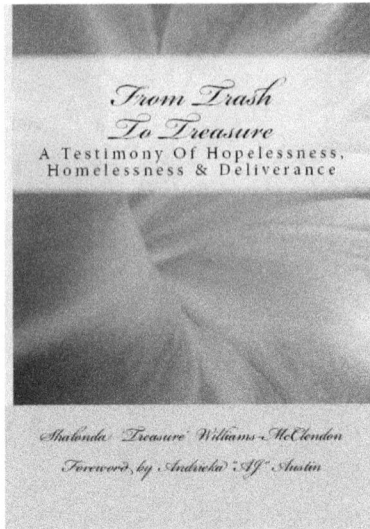

From Trash
To Treasure
A Testimony Of Hopelessness,
Homelessness & Deliverance

Shalonda "Treasure" Williams-McClendon
Foreword by Andreka "AJ" Austin

Order your copy of "From Trash To Treasure: Testimony of Hopelessness, Homelessness and Deliverance" and get it at a discounted price just for purchasing this book! :D

You can only get it at
www.TheInspirationalTreasure.com/FTTT

Shhhh … keep this link to yourself but feel free to share this book purchasing information.

I love you just because I can,

Prophetess Shalonda "Treasure" Williams
The Nspirational Treasure

CPSIA information can be obtained
at www.ICGtesting.com
Printed in the USA
BVHW041751010520
579053BV00010B/1421

9 781795 453110